The Macmillan Pre-Vocational Series

Series editor
Douglas Pride

Core Skills in Manufacture

Contributors

David Draycott
Jeffrey Forbes
Derek Miles
Lawrence Miles
David Stevens
Terry Withington

Macmillan Education

Acknowledgements

The contributors and publishers wish to thank Judith Irving and Norman Smith for permission to reproduce Information Page B, pp. 59–64, taken from *Core Skills in Communication*; Trainwell YTS (West Bromwich) and staff at the Polytechnic, Wolverhampton, for their help with the photographs; and Christine Broome, for typing the manuscript.

The contributors and publishers wish to acknowledge the following photograph sources: Austin Rover Group Ltd, p. 15; British Gas Corporation, p. 48; illustration on p. 71 reproduced by kind permission of British Telecom Yellow Pages; Jim Brownbill, pp. 36, 49; Camera Press, pp. 33, 38; Ron Chapman, p. 44; Consumer's Association, p. 69; HMSO, pp. 51, 73; illustration on p. 67 taken from the *Readers Digest Repair Manual*, used with permission; illustrations on pp. 66 and 68 used by kind permission of Shell from *The Shell Book of How Cars Work;* Town and Planning Publications, p. 32; Derick Webster, pp. 18, 20, 22, 27, 28, 39, 42, 46, 52, 53.

First published 1988

Published by
MACMILLAN EDUCATION LTD
Houndmills, Basingstoke, Hampshire RG21 2XS and London
Companies and representatives throughout the world

Printed in Hong Kong

British Library Cataloguing in Publication Data
Withington, Terry
Core Skills in Manufacture. — (The Macmillan pre-vocational series.)
1. Manufacturing processes
I. Title
670   TS149
ISBN 0–333–42533–2

Contents

Introductory assignments

Exploratory assignments

Information pages

Introduction

This series is designed to help students meet the criteria laid down by the Joint Board for the new Certificate of Pre-Vocational Education. It aims to fulfil the three main requirements of CPVE courses:

(a) the integration of a core of basic skills with a wide-ranging choice of vocational studies;
(b) activity-based learning; and
(c) a flexibility that enables courses to be tailored to the needs of individual students.

The books in the series are arranged in two groups: one group concentrates on developing the main core competences, using different vocational settings; the other concentrates on the skills required in the vocational categories (the CPVE introductory and exploratory modules), but also provides practice in the core competences.

Each book consists of twenty assignments which develop skills in both general and specific vocational contexts. Ten of these concentrate on skills in general vocational contexts and ten on specific vocational situations (see diagram).

Main core competences	Core Skills in Communication	Core Skills in Numeracy	Core Skills in Industrial, Social and Environmental Studies	Core Skills in Science and Technology	Core Skills in Information Technology
	10 Core assignments (general vocational contexts) 10 Focus assignments (specific vocational situations) 10 Information pages				

Course

Vocational skills	10 Introductory assignments (general vocational contexts) 10 Exploratory assignments (specific vocational situations) 10 Information pages						
	Core Skills in Business and Administrative Services	Core Skills in Information Technology and Micro-electronic Systems	Core Skills in Service Engineering	Core Skills in Manufacture	Core Skills in Craft-based Activities	Core Skills in Distribution	Core Skills in Services to People

The assignments are free-standing and can be combined in different modular ways according to individual course needs. To assist selection and combination, the objectives of each assignment are given both at its head and in a grid at the beginning of each book. At the end of each book information pages give facts and advice to support the activities in the assignments.

Core Skills in Manufacture has ten introductory assignments which develop awareness of the inter-related issues involved in manufacturing through contexts related to the industrial activities of the surrounding community. The ten exploratory assignments concentrate more specifically on the main vocational categories, and encourage students to tackle the problems which face manufacturers through a variety of assignment types including direct involvement with local industries and investigations into the impact of new technology on the production of manufactured goods. Ten information pages provide guidance on matters of fact, research and design.

The material in the volume is also useful for YTS off-the-job training, the National Certificate (Scotland), BTEC/City and Guilds pre-vocational courses and City and Guilds Specific Skills Schemes.

CPVE grid

Assignments	Personal and Career Development	Industrial, Social and Environmental Studies	Communication	Social Skills	Numeracy	Science and Technology	Information Technology	Creative Development	Practical Skills	Problem-solving
1 Work out	■		■	■				■		■
2 Who makes what?	■	■	■				■			■
3 Play it safe	■	■	■				■			■
4 New technology	■	■	■			■				
5 How is it made?	■				■	■				
6 Old and new	■					■				
7 Stop the rust		■				■				
8 Safe check	■	■		■					■	
9 Safe and sound	■			■					■	
10 Summing it up	■			■	■				■	
11 Out and about	■			■			■			
12 MOT		■								
13 New technology in action	■		■			■				
14 Customer complaints	■		■	■						■
15 Shape up	■					■			■	■
16 A bench for all seasons	■		■			■				
17 Save your energy		■		■						
18 Mushroom-growing	■	■				■		■		
19 Spillage	■	■								■
20 Packaging problems	■		■		■			■		■

Introductory assignments

Work out

To develop your understanding of
- the manufacturing process
- the different processes used in manufacture

Introduction

Manufacturing means making things. Look around your classroom, home or neighbourhood and you will see manufactured objects. All will have been designed, and they will have been produced in a wide range of ways. The *processes* of manufacturing also will have been designed. The companies that are doing well have the right process for the product.

No matter how large or how small a manufacturing company is, it will need to decide how to carry out its manufacturing process. There are different ways of organising the work. Different ways of producing the same product have different advantages and disadvantages, and what may seem the most obvious and best way of making a single item may not be the best way of producing a large number of those items.

This assignment asks you to compare two methods which are frequently used.

Task 1

With the other members of your group, decide on a very simple product. An example might be a small notepad. It would need a cover, perhaps with a design printed or drawn on it; a number of pages; and some way of fastening the whole thing together, such as stapling.

Task 2

When you have decided, find space so that each of you can make one version of the chosen product in your own way. Do not watch how the others are making theirs.

Compare your products when you have finished, and discuss exactly how each one was made. As a group, choose the one that you like the best and write down exactly how it was made.

Task 3

The next step is to make a number of the products – say 10. You will need to work out how much material, paper and so on you need, and arrange for this to be available.

Divide the group into two and share the materials out between you. Each group will make half of the products. Choose one member of each group to act as an organiser and also to keep an exact record of the problems and successes of the group.

Group 1   Each person will make one complete product. The organiser should explain to each person how this is done, and ensure that the products are similar and usable. Group 2 will judge the product quality.

Group 2   Each person will make only one section or element of each product. For example, if the group were making the notepad, then one person could print or draw the cover design on the covers for all of the pads, another person could cut up all of the paper, and so on. Group 1 will judge the product quality.

Task 4

While each group is completing the agreed number of products, the organiser must note:

(a) the total time taken;
(b) the time taken to train the group;
(c) the materials used;
(d) any wastage;
(e) any problems;
(f) the advantages of this method of production;
(g) the disadvantages of this method of production.

Task 5

When the products are complete, the two groups should swap their products and carry out the process of evaluation. Use the table shown in Figure 1.

Figure 1 Product evaluation

Criteria	Marks	1–10	1–10	1–10	1–10
Neatness					
Attractiveness					
Fitness for purpose					
Other comments					

Task 6

Group 1 and Group 2 should now meet together again and discuss the notes made by the organisers and the evaluations made by the groups. Group 1 should draw together conclusions about their method of manufacture; Group 2 should do the same about theirs.

Each group should then make up a wall chart that explains what they did and how they did it. They should attach an example of the finished product.

2

Who makes what?

—————AIM—————

To develop your
- awareness of the range of manufacturing products and processes
- ability to identify categories
- ability to record and catalogue information

Introduction

As you study manufacture, you will be carrying out projects, looking for jobs and going on work experience. You will find it useful to have information readily available on local manufacturers and their products, in the form of a comprehensive and well-catalogued list. You will also need to keep this catalogue up to date, making additions and deletions as circumstances change.

This assignment may more easily be carried out by a group than by one person, because of the amount of information to be processed. If you decide to work as a group you will need to allocate individual responsibilities in the tasks.

Task 1

Make a list of raw materials which might be used in manufacturing processes — metals, wood, plastics, clay, leather, etc. Put together some ideas of the kinds of products which could be made locally with these raw materials. You will probably know of some already.

Task 2

With your list use your local *Yellow Pages*, industrial and commercial *Yellow Pages* and, if you can, your local Chamber of Industry and Commerce's Directory to identify manufacturers who use those raw materials to make their products. Note their names, addresses and telephone numbers. (Remember that you are interested only in *manufacturers*, not in suppliers of manufactured goods or in providers of services.)

Task 3

Now decide upon a method of storing the information you have assembled. A card index might be one way. Figure 1 shows one card from such an index. Alternatively, if you have access to a computer, you could feed your information into a computer program. Whatever method you choose you will need to consider the cost of setting up the system, and how easy it will be with this system to access and update the information.

Figure 1 A card from a card index

Category: Metal

Firm   Address

BAINES LTD.   GREEN LANE
                                                      WESTBOROUGH
                                                      WE9 4AJ

Product   Telephone

SMALL-LINK CHAIN   WESTBOROUGH 8941

Task 4

At the moment the information you have is very basic. Choose two or three manufacturing firms for further study. Find out, for example:

(a) How long has the firm been in business?
(b) How many employees does it have?
(c) What is the range of its products?
(d) Does the firm supply a catalogue to customers?
(e) Where does it mainly sell its products, and to whom?

You will have to make contact with these manufacturers either by telephone or by letter. Arrange to visit them if possible.

————IMPORTANT————

Read this information page:
D Sources of
   information

Task 5

Look at your record system as it stands. How easy would it be to add to your basic records the information you found out in Task 4?

3 Play it safe

AIM

To develop your

- knowledge and awareness of the likely dangers in manufacturing industry
- ability to identify particular roles and the effect which they have on behaviour
- ability to work co-operatively to solve problems
- social and communication skills

Introduction

It is essential for all who work in manufacturing industry to be able to deal with, and take responsibility for, health and safety at work. Workers must also be able to co-operate with others when problems and potential dangers arise, and be ready to take measures to resolve the problems.

In this assignment you are asked to imagine that you work at DMC Engineering Ltd, a small engineering company making parts and components for the motor vehicle industry. You will be using the skills required to deal with hazards at work, and will carry out a role-play with your tutor and fellow students.

Task 1

Your first task is to collect as much information as you can about the kinds of dangers and hazards which could possibly occur in an engineering plant.

You will have some ideas on this already, but to increase your knowledge of this aspect of engineering it would be useful to arrange for a person with expert knowledge and experience in this area to visit your school or college and talk to your group. You will first need to consider the possible experts in this field, such as trade union officials, managers of local companies, and officials from your local council. When you have decided who to invite, write a letter proposing the visit. Make clear what you want the speaker to talk about.

Figure 1 Background information

> ## THE SITUATION
>
> The section of the plant in which you work produces finished parts from cast aluminium and metal bars of various grades. There is much heavy lifting involved, and the machinery you use includes centre and capstan lathes, vertical drilling machines, grinders, and presses.
>
> Over the past year complaints have circulated amongst your workmates concerning safety standards in the workshop. There have been many minor accidents and recently two serious health and safety incidents.
>
> Also there is general dissatisfaction with the workshop foreperson. There is a strong feeling that complaints about accidents and general safety standards are not taken up when made.

Figure 2 Your role

> ## ROLE CARD
>
> You work for DMC Engineering. You need to make the following choices about the role you wish to play:
> 1 What is your job?
> 2 What machinery or equipment do you operate? What are its likely dangers?
> 3 What is your attitude to health and safety and the situation in the plant?
> 4 What type of character do you wish to play?

Task 2

Read Figure 1, which describes the problems at DMC Engineering Ltd.

In response to this situation, you organise a short meeting of the employees in your section. Everyone who is to attend the meeting should read Figure 2 and choose a role.

Choose someone to act as secretary to the meeting. Using the information you have gained from your visiting speaker, discuss the dangers and hazards in the plant and list them. Then, as a group, write a letter of complaint about health and safety to the company manager. Ask for an open meeting between management and all the employees in your section.

Task 3

You are now going to hold the meeting with management.

Brief your tutor and ask him or her to play the role of the company manager. Give your tutor the letter of complaint. Arrange the time and place of the open meeting.

Task 4

Choose one member of the group to chair the meeting. Then discuss the issues with the manager until you reach a solution to the problems. All employees can speak on the issues, in an orderly fashion.

The solutions agreed should be written down and signed by both sides as a binding agreement.

Task 5

When you have carried out the role-play, discuss amongst yourselves how effectively you dealt with the problems in the plant.

Having carried out the role-play, you may wish to do it again to explore alternative ways of dealing with the problems. It might be useful to video the role-play and discuss it after watching it as a group.

————IMPORTANT————

Read these information pages:
E Health and safety
F Role-playing

4 New technology

———— AIM ————

AIM

To develop your
- skills in writing effectively
- ability to present information
- awareness of the roles of new technology

Introduction

We hear a great deal about robots building cars and about computers taking over the work of people. Often robots are shown in advertising films, where they may look like strange metal people. Yet real robots in industry do not look like humans. They tend to stay in one place, doing repetitive tasks. Often they simply carry forward the progress already seen in the automation of production lines.

Robots will be used more and more, and it is important that anyone wanting to work in manufacturing has a clear and realistic idea of what robots can and cannot do. For this assignment you will need to visit local manufacturing companies to collect information about the uses of new technology in the workplace. You will make a presentation of this information, giving a clear idea of the applications, and the advantages and disadvantages to the companies visited. You should also give visual examples of each of these elements.

Read through *all* the tasks before you begin.

Task 1

With the other members of your group, discuss the companies in your area which are likely to have installed new technological equipment. Write letters to the most likely ones, asking if they would be willing to be involved with your assignment. Explain to them what you want to do.

Task 2

When you have received replies from these firms, draw up a list of the activities needed to complete the project and decide who is going to carry out each activity. Write this down so that you can refer to it later. Make appointments for the visits to firms that have offered to help.

Task 3

If you have access to video equipment you will be able to use this for the assignment, but a camera and an audio tape-recorder can also be used.

In your group, first discuss the format of the finished presentation. Remember that it should show both the advantages and the disadvantages of the new equipment being used. You will need to plan your presentation thoroughly so that you have a clear idea of how it will look.

Television programmes, whether they use still or moving pictures, are carefully planned in great detail. You will not be able to write down exactly who or what will be in each camera shot, but the overall plan, timing and balance should be designed before you start. See Figure 1.

Figure 1 A plan for a video or tape/slide presentation

SECTION	SUBJECT	LOCATION	TIMING	WHO DOES WHAT
Intro	Group	Classroom	1 minute	Carol & Jane
Interview	Manager	Office	3 minutes	David: Questions 1-13
Visuals	Robots	Shop floor	1 minute	Stuart: Voice-over
Interview	Supervisor	Office?	2 minutes	Sarah: Questions 14-22 (previous working practice)
Visuals	Close-ups (e.g. computer programmer)	Around workshop	1 minute	Jasmia: Voice-over

Task 4

Compile the list of questions that you intend to ask the managers, supervisors and operators. Decide on the pictures or video sequences that you particularly want, and make sure someone is ready to note the details in writing as each shot is taken.

Now visit the firms as arranged. Remember that the people you meet are all busy: they will probably be able to give you only a short time. Try to find operators who remember how the jobs were carried out previously, so that people who see the final presentation can understand how the production system has changed.

Task 5

Assemble the interviews and film or stills into the final presentation.

_____IMPORTANT_____

Read this information page:
I Computer uses

Task 6

Show your video or tape/slide presentation to another group, and discuss your work with them.

5 How is it made?

AIM

To develop your
- awareness of individual tasks within manufacturing processes
- ability to produce diagrams and flowcharts
- communication skills

Introduction

In manufacturing industries each worker is likely to be involved in only one task out of the hundreds needed to produce a single product. In the fashion trades, for example, one employee might spend all his or her time cutting cloth, while another may carry out only the final pressing or packing.

This assignment is designed to help you understand the manufacturing process as a whole. It will help you to see how the individual tasks performed by different people result in the production of a complete product.

In completing the tasks below you will become familiar with all the processes and tasks involved in making a simple garment. By taking it apart and then investigating how it was made and sold, you will understand the fashion industry as a set of inter-related activities.

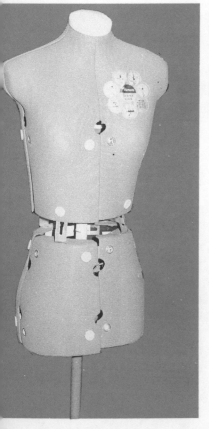

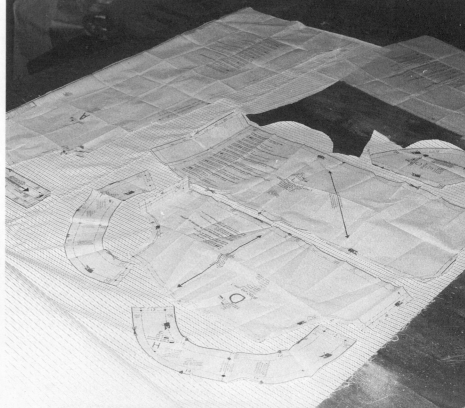

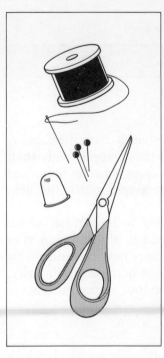

Task 1

Consider the different types of garment worn. Try to find one that is made in your local area.

Now find an example of this garment, one that you can obtain at little or no cost — perhaps an old pair of trousers or a skirt you or a member of your family no longer wants. Make a detailed drawing of it, showing the back and front views and all measurements.

Task 2

To find out more about the garment your next task is carefully to take it apart. Make sure you don't tear or lose any of the material.

Make detailed notes about how it was made. Identify:

(a) the type of fabric and its likely country of origin;
(b) the quantity of basic material used, and also the haberdashery used (cotton, lace, zips, etc.);
(c) the likely cost of the cloth and haberdashery.

Task 3

Construct a flowchart to show the stages of production. List the tasks involved at each stage. The best way to approach this is to decide what *you* would do if you yourself were making the garment.

Task 4

It would help to compare what you have worked out in Task 3 with the actual processes and tasks used in making garments of the kind you have chosen.

Identify a firm in your local area that makes this garment. Write a letter or make a telephone call to arrange a visit.

Then, before you make the visit, prepare a checklist of things to find out. You might need to ask about:

(a) laying the cloth;
(b) cutting the cloth;
(c) stages in machining;
(d) fitting;
(e) decoration;
(f) labelling, packing, and boxing;
(g) selling and distribution.

IMPORTANT

Read these information pages:
C Presenting information
D Sources of information
G Using flowcharts

Task 5

After your visit, write a report comparing what you found out about making the garment in the factory and what you discovered when you took the garment apart. How did the stages and processes of production in the factory differ from the way you yourself would have made the garment? Present your report to your group, using charts and diagrams to illustrate your findings.

6 Old and new

To develop your
awareness of
- how manufacturing
  processes evolve
- the advantages and
  disadvantages of
  different
  manufacturing
  processes

Introduction

The way in which things are made is constantly changing. Many manufacturers say in the literature which they supply with their products that they may modify the product from time to time, and that the description in the literature may no longer match the item bought.

Although manufacturers change the product to improve it, there are other possible reasons for changes. Sometimes different materials are used in order to reduce costs; in other cases new manufacturing methods become available which reduce waste or increase productivity.

This assignment gives you an opportunity to look at products made by old and new manufacturing methods.

Task 1

Find old examples of products which are still made today. Look in museums, junk shops or jumble sales, or ask older members of your community. Old people have an enormous fund of information about the past, and some will have been employed in manufacturing industries over half a century ago. This resource will be particularly useful in compiling a list of products that would be suitable for further investigation.

Enter your examples in a table like that shown in Figure 1.

Figure 1 Table of old products

OLD EXAMPLE OF A PRODUCT STILL AVAILABLE	MADE OF? MADE HOW?
Washing-up bowl	Pressed steel with baked enamel coating
Carpet	Woven in wool by steam-driven machinery

Task 2

Look for new examples of the same products and make a similar table (Figure 2).

Figure 2 Table of new products

NEW EXAMPLE OF PRODUCT	MADE OF? MADE HOW?
Washing-up bowl	Impact-moulded plastic
Carpet	Nylon, tufted into foam-rubber back

Task 3

Take any *one* item that interests you and make a more detailed study of the old manufacturing processes. Try to identify *why* changes were introduced — for example because of the development of new materials or processes, or because of increased costs of the raw materials. For some products it may be possible to arrange a visit to a manufacturer who has been involved in both types of production: this would help you to understand the reasons for change.

Write a short report of your findings.

_____IMPORTANT_____

Read these information pages:
A Properties of materials
B Social-survey techniques
D Sources of information

Task 4

What do the public think? Draw up a list of questions which you could ask passers-by in the street. What manufactured goods are now less well-made than they used to be? Which show a big improvement?

Keep your questions simple. Use a word processor or typewriter to produce a smarter, more professional-looking questionnaire.

Prepare a short presentation of your findings for your school or college class.

7

Stop the rust

———— AIM ————

To develop your
- skills in writing reports
- problem-solving skills
- ability to search for information
- awareness of safe techniques

Introduction

Almost all metals used in manufacturing will eventually become corroded. The rate of corrosion varies with the type of metal. Irons and steel corrode quickly, whereas copper and tin corrode very slowly.

Corrosion can be prevented by coating the surface with some form of protection, such as paint. One well-known example of metal being painted for protection is the Forth Road Bridge in Scotland, which has provided many people with employment over many years. It is said that when the painters finally reach the end of the Forth Bridge it is time to start again at the other end!

Paint is not always adequate as a protection. The salt used on roads during the winter weather causes rapid rusting even of the most protected car surfaces.

This assignment asks you to find out how metal surfaces on cars have been protected against corrosion. You will start by looking at repair methods, and then investigate the method of manufacture.

Task 1

The tasks listed in Figure 1 must all be carried out in repairing a damaged car body section. The list, however, is not in the correct order. Re-order the tasks to show the correct method of repairing a damaged area.

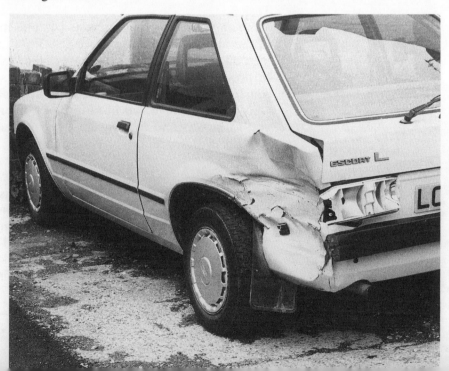

Figure 1 Tasks in damage repair

1 Rub down with rough wet-and-dry paper
2 Apply a coat of primer paint
3 Wipe the surface clean
4 Remove all loose particles
5 Rub down with medium wet-and-dry paper
6 Apply top coats
7 Polish the surface
8 Apply undercoats
9 Rub down with fine wet-and-dry paper
10 Rinse the area with clean water
11 Allow the paint to dry for at least two weeks
12 Apply wax polish
13 Apply body filler
14 Wait for the surface to dry completely
15 Remove the old paint from the area
16 Scratch the surface to provide a 'key' for the filler paste

Task 2

Collect some manufacturers' catalogues which explain vehicle finishing and the techniques involved. You could visit some car sales for popular makes of vehicle.

Use these documents to compare the different manufacturers' methods of protecting surfaces. Try to include in your material some examples of a high-quality manufacture: these will give you a basis for comparison of your findings. Report on your findings.

Task 3

In addition to the vehicle paint protection given by the manufacturers, there are firms who offer rust-proofing by such techniques as 'under-sealing' and 'spray-sealing'. Use *Yellow Pages* and motoring magazines to find out what this extra protection is and add this to your report.

Task 4

The use of paints always carries with it workshop hazards. Consider the special hazards in bodywork repair, and make a detailed report of these.

———IMPORTANT———

Read these information pages:
A Properties of materials
E Health and safety

Task 5

With the safety report from Task 4 in mind, sketch a safety poster suitable for display in a body workshop. The poster should be eye-catching and should be designed to reduce accidents by explaining how to use paint safely.

8 Safe check

——— AIM ———

To develop your
- ability to identify hazards
- ability to report hazards
- knowledge of health and safety procedures

Introduction

In this assignment you will look at standard safety signs which relate to manufacturing premises and to health and safety issues in general. Safety signs follow these general rules:

- a circle with a diagonal red bar on a white background means you *must not do* something;
- a triangle with a black rim on a yellow background *warns* or *cautions* you about something;
- a blue circle means you *must do* something.

Safety signs are provided by the Royal Society for the Prevention of Accidents (ROSPA). You can buy signs from the Society.

You will be able to carry out this assignment in your school or college, but it could also be a work-based project.

Task 1

Identify the safety signs in use in the workrooms where manufacture-related activities take place. Make a note of each sign and its location (Figure 1). Also record any signs which you think ought to be displayed and are not.

Figure 1 Record of safety signs

SIGN	LOCATIONS
Eye protection must be worn	Engineering workshop Carpentry workshop Welding workshop Gas installation workshop

Task 2

Make a safety audit of the manufacture-based rooms in your school or college. You will need to decide on a format of the checklist and the headings you are going to use (see Figure 2). Decide which items you are going to include in your audit. You might consider:

- fire appliances and fire procedures;
- exits and entrances;
- guards on machinery;
- first-aid equipment;
- lighting and heating;
- ventilation.

Figure 2 Safety audit   You will be able to think of others.

ROOM:	ENGINEERING 2			
HAZARD		YES	NO	COMMENTS
Floor:	Is it free of obstacles?	✓		
	Is the surface even and non-slip?		✓	Floor near centre lathe is wearing and uneven.
	Is it free of waste?		✓	A lot of swarf round lathes 2 and 3.

———IMPORTANT———

Read these information pages:
C Presenting information
E Health and safety

Task 3

When you have made your audit, present a report of your findings to an appropriate tutor, together with any recommendations for improvement of health and safety practice.

Task 4

Design a poster to show the importance of observing safety signs.

9 Safe and sound

———— AIM ————

To develop your
- skills in undertaking practical tests of equipment
- knowledge of protective clothing and equipment
- understanding of safety standards

Introduction

Too many accidents still happen in the workplace as a result of workers failing to use the proper protective clothing and equipment. In this assignment you will survey current practice in your school or college. Although the assignment is college- or school-based, it could be done in a workplace as well; the actual tasks could easily be adapted to be carried out during work experience.

If you wish to extend your knowledge about protective clothing and equipment, contact industrial suppliers in your area. They usually appear in *Yellow Pages* under 'Industrial Safety Clothing' or 'Safety Equipment'. Suppliers normally offer catalogues and price lists which you might find useful in this assignment.

Welding is used below as the example in the tasks, but the method would be the same for *any* manufacturing area you study.

Task 1

Visit the sections of your school or college where manufacturing-related work takes place — engineering, pottery, dressmaking, woodworking and so on. Record the protective clothing and equipment in use, as in Figure 1.

Figure 1 Protective clothing and equipment

DEPARTMENT	ROOM	PROTECTIVE CLOTHING AND EQUIPMENT
Welding	E.3	Overalls Face masks Goggles Gloves Safety shoes

Task 2

(a) Find out which of the equipment is provided for students, and what the students have to provide for themselves.
(b) Find out the cost of individual items of clothing and equipment, and make a list of these.

Task 3

Check some of the equipment and clothing to see how comfortable it is to work in. Devise a checklist like that in Figure 2.

Note also items which would be *unsuitable*. For example, would you wear a nylon overall if you were welding? If not, why not?

Figure 2 Using protective equipment and clothing

Clothing/ Equipment	Comfortable		Adjustable		Comments
	YES	NO	YES	NO	
Welding handshield					Awkward to hold and weld. Only use for a short time.
Gloves					Very flexible.
Welding helmet					A bit warm, but leaves both hands free.

Task 4

(a) How do you know whether the protective clothing and equipment is up to standard? In the illustration in Figure 3 you will see the safety triangle under the visor, with 'BS 1542' printed below it. What does 'BS' stand for? If you don't know, find out its meaning, its origin, who awards it and why.

(b) Check whether the BS triangle appears on the protective equipment and clothing in use in your school or college.

Figure 3 A safety visor

Task 5

(a) Put together an information sheet which describes particular job roles and the kind of protective clothing and equipment which a student could expect to use either in school/college or on a work-experience project (Figure 4).

Figure 4 Jobs and clothing or equipment

Job	Clothing/equipment	Provider
Welder	Full overall/boiler suit − cotton drill	Often the worker
	Gloves − leather; cotton; chrome; leather latex	Employer
	Helmet − glass-fibre; shade filter	Employer

————IMPORTANT————

Read these information pages:
C Presenting information
E Health and safety
H Technical terms

(b) You might like to put up a visual display including photographs or sketches which illustrate your information sheets.

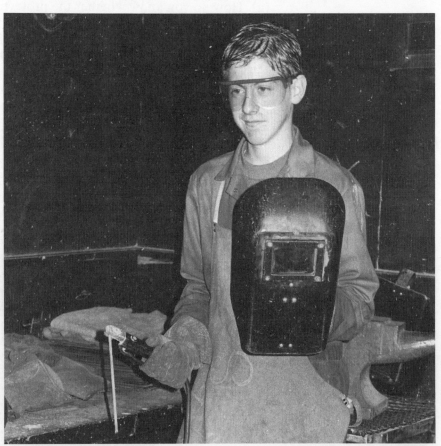

10 Summing it up

―――――AIM―――――

To develop your skills in
- planning tasks
- costing and pricing tasks
- presenting numerical information

Introduction

Everything has a cost, and if all of the costs involved in the manufacture of a product are not taken into account then the company could make a loss and eventually go bankrupt.

For this assignment you will need to have the facilities to make something yourself — it might be a garment, a piece of pottery, or something made in wood or metal. The choice will depend on the equipment and materials available to you.

Although the manufacture is important, this assignment is about all the costs, including hidden costs, of the item that you are making. You will need to calculate not just the costs of equipment and materials, but also the running costs — for example, the cost of using electricity. Planning will be important, as will the ability to find out the actual costs of the materials you are using. Before you start, make sure that these things are possible.

Task 1

Decide on the item that you are going to make. Prepare a detailed plan, showing all of the materials, equipment and facilities that you will need in order to make it. Go through the process in your mind step by step, and try to make sure that you do not leave anything out. (You can add extra things later as you think of them.)

Task 2

Check that all of the items on your list are available to you. Mark clearly those items which require additional expenses. (For example, if you use an electric iron you also use electricity.)

Then, write down the sequence of events in the order that they will take place. Try to estimate how long you think each part of the process is going to take. Include time for glues to set or for hot materials to cool down, and so on. When you have finished you will be ready to compare your estimates with the actual times.

Task 3

Make the item that you have chosen, timing each stage. You will need a stopwatch to time your activities accurately. Measure or weigh each component and keep careful records.

You may only be able to find out the cost of larger quantities than you actually use: if so you will have to calculate the cost of what you use. For example, you may find the cost of using electrical equipment per hour and divide this by 60 to calculate the cost per minute.

COSTING: Pillowcase			
ITEM	UNIT COST (per metre, per hour, etc.)	AMOUNT USED	COST
White cotton			
Polyester thread			
Sewing machine			

Figure 1 Costing analysis

_____IMPORTANT_____

Read these information pages:
C Presenting
   information
J Costs

Task 4

Draw up a chart of the materials used in the process and the costs involved (Figure 1). Then do the same thing for the *time* that you have used. Find out from a local firm or Job Centre the rate per hour for this work, and calculate the cost of your work.

When you have completed all of your calculations, compare them with your estimates and calculate the final cost of the product.

Task 5

Present your product with its full costing analysis, perhaps as a chart or a booklet. Show how you made the item and how you calculated the costs.

Exploratory assignments

11

To develop your abilities in
- collecting and organising information
- communicating effectively in a range of situations

Introduction

Company visits are becoming increasingly common in schools and colleges. Often they are interesting and enjoyable, and you learn about the work of the company. Members of the company learn about you, too, and about your course.

Usually company visits yield a lot of information, but it is not easy to pass this on to other students who might be interested. In this assignment your group will make several company visits and you will organise and store the information you collect.

Read through all the tasks before you start.

Task 1

Divide into sub-groups of 4–6 people, each with a common interest in a particular area of manufacture.

Using industrial directories, *Yellow Pages*, local newpaper advertisements and so on, identify companies who specialise in your chosen area of manufacture. At the end you need one company for each member of the sub-group.

You are going to make a company study. In 15 minutes, brainstorm as many items of information as you can that you could find out about the company. Think of things that would be useful in planning a company visit or a work-experience project.

Task 2

Compile a master checklist of items. Group the items to match the stages of the study, such as:

- preparation before the visit;
- the visit;
- follow-up work after the visit.

Appoint one member of your sub-group to report back to the whole group. Compare the master checklists produced by the various sub-groups, and make alterations to your own if you wish.

Task 3

Now work individually.

Select one of the companies identified by your sub-group. You are going to arrange for your sub-group to visit this company.

Plan to make the best possible use of the visit. Do any of your

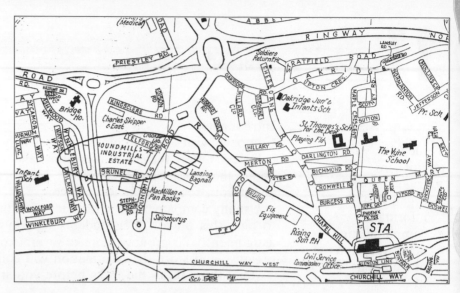

group want to work in this area? Is there a particular process you want to see, or a particular person, such as a young trainee?

(a) Create your own checklist from the master checklist — you may need more specific information about that particular company.
(b) Contact the company to arrange a visit. You may telephone the company initially, but at some point you should write, saying why you want to visit, explaining what you hope to find out, and asking for dates and times that would be convenient.
(c) When you are offered a date and time, check with other members of your sub-group that it does not clash with another visit. Try to spread the visits out over a suitable period of time.
(d) Write back to confirm the visit.

Task 4
Find out about the company. How many employees has it? How and where does it operate? You could ask for this information when you first write to the company (Task 3), or perhaps you could find it in a directory.

Present this information to the sub-group as a *briefing note*. Make clear which company the note refers to and when the visit will take place.

The company representative may be equally interested in you and your group. Put together a briefing note for him or her, giving relevant information about your school/college, your course and your project.

Task 5
From your checklist, prepare a list of questions to ask during the visit. Perhaps you will have an interview as part of the visit, or

perhaps you will have to ask the questions as you go around. Put a box against each question, so that you can tick it when it has been answered.

Task 6
Now make the visit.

You are the leader for the visit you have arranged. There shouldn't be much to do if you have arranged it fully. You will probably do most of the talking — other members of the group will support you and ask questions of their own. Don't forget to record what you are told.

Task 7
You — and the other sub-groups — now have a lot of information about a lot of companies.

Meet together as a sub-group. Discuss how you could record this information as a database. Will you organise the information alphabetically, or by geographical area, or by kind of manufacture?

Report back to the whole group (as in Task 2) and agree a method of storing the information that suits all of you. Then create the database.

Task 8
Finally, don't forget to write back to the companies thanking them for their help. You might like to say something about what you learnt from the visit, or what you did afterwards. As a result of your work in Task 7, you may also have new questions to ask.

_____IMPORTANT_____
Read these information pages:
C Presenting
   information
D Sources of
   information
I Computer uses

12 MOT

To develop your
skills in
- making decisions
  based on information
- problem-solving
- presenting
  information in a
  graphic form

Introduction

There is a constant need to control the cost of manufacture, and
engineers are always on the lookout to ensure that the production
line is designed to be as efficient as possible.

The purpose of a production line is simple: to ensure that processes
are carried out in a logical and coherent order which will produce the
manufactured goods cost-effectively. This assignment asks you to
consider a common process and break it down into logical tasks
which can be carried out in sequence. As you do so you will gain an
insight into the flow-line process.

Task 1

Consider the lists in Figure 1 which contain items that need to be
checked during the MOT test. Place these items into logical lists in an
order which can be checked by engineers. Give each list a general
heading.

Figure 1 MOT checks

List 1	List 2
1 Main braking system	16 Tyre condition
2 Rear lamps	17 Headlamp aim
3 Steering controls	18 Windscreen wipers
4 Steering mechanism	19 Parking brake efficiency
5 Parking brakes	20 Wheel bearings
6 Tyre types	21 Suspension
7 Road wheels	22 Windscreen washers
8 Horn	23 Stop lamps
9 Headlamps	24 Shock absorbers
10 Direction indicators	25 Rear reflectors
11 Vehicle structure	26 Steering assembly
12 Seat belt operation	27 Security of seat mountings
13 Main brake efficiency	28 Exhaust system
14 Silencer	29 Balance of braking system
15 Condition of seat belts	30 Dip lamp operation

Task 2

Read the consultants' brief in Figure 2.

Consider the sketch of the garage at the present time (Figure 2) and
make recommendations on where checking of the vehicle will take

Figure 2 The situation

The Consultants' Brief

You are part of a team of consultants who have been employed to complete a contract for a small town-based garage. The garage, 'Mile Sure', has until now been a general repair workshop, but it has seen its share of the market fall due to competition from new garages in the area and increasing numbers of drivers doing DIY repairs.

Recently the shareholders met and took the advice of the garage foreman to move their work into fast MOT testing which relies on a large turnover of tests at a very low cost to the motorist. They hope that a garage that only carries out MOT tests will be viewed as a trustworthy firm which can be relied upon to give an unbiased opinion of the vehicle, rather than as a firm which is looking for the repairs from failed MOT tests. The foreman has carried out a market survey which convinced the shareholders of the need to change.

Your team of consultants has been asked to present recommendations to the garage owners on the introduction of a flow-line MOT garage. The accompanying sketch indicates the current arrangement of the garage.

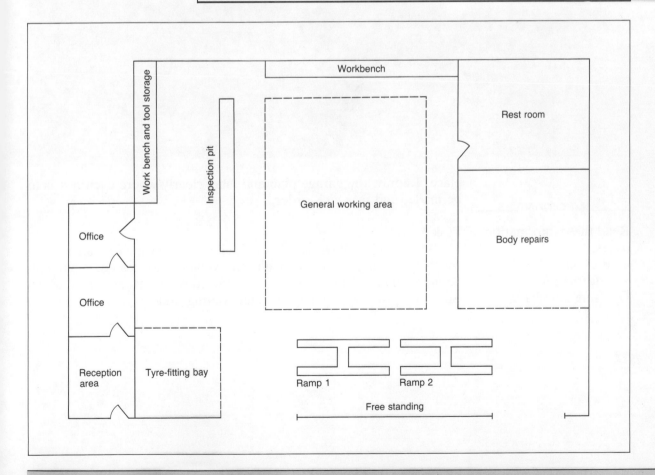

place. Redraw the garage plan and label clearly where each test is to be made, and in which order.

——— IMPORTANT ———

Read these information pages:
C Presenting information
G Using flowcharts

Task 3
The shareholders have asked especially that you include an area in which the owners can wait while the vehicles are tested. Your recommendations should include any furniture or other items which would be provided in the customer waiting area.

13 New technology in action

_____ AIM _____

To develop your
awareness of
• the impact of new
  technology on
  industry and business
• the uses of new
  technology in
  manufacture

Introduction

In order to stay competitive, many companies have now installed computerised production equipment. From conveyor belts making biscuits to coal mines you will find computers in control of processes, with supervisors present simply to check that everything is working smoothly.

There is a lot of confusion about the capabilities of computers and about their roles in manufacturing. In some companies the designer's plans for a product may be converted directly into the production-line process which might be fully automatic. In others, a computer might run only one lathe. This assignment gives you the opportunity to analyse one installation and carry out a technical case study of new technology in action.

Task 1

Identify a large manufacturing company which specialises in making computer-aided manufacturing equipment. You could check through reference books in the library, or you might find it easier to ask a local company that uses computers in its manufacturing process for details of its supplier.

Task 2

Draw up a plan of your case study, listing the different elements that you will be trying to find out about. These might include questions such as these:

• What do the computers actually do?
• What sort of computers are in use?
• Who programs their actions?
• How many workers did they replace?
• What hours do they work?
• How often do they break down?
• How much do they cost to buy or lease?
• What are the maintenance costs?
• Which processes are not computerised?
• Are there any further plans for computerisation?
• What are the main features of the system used?
• Who trains the workers to use this equipment?

Your task is to find out as much as you can. The more thoroughly you *plan* your study, the easier it will be to carry out.

Task 3

Contact the computer manufacturing company identified in Task 1 and explain your assignment. Ask the company to select one piece of equipment they make which is particularly useful in computer-aided manufacturing, and to send you information about it.

Task 4

Now arrange to make a number of visits to the computer manufacturing company; or, better, to a local firm that uses the chosen equipment. It would be most helpful to see the production facilities in action.

When you visit, make sketches, take photographs, and talk to some of the people involved with the computerised production − the production manager, the supervisor, an operator, a programmer, and so on. Ask them all as many questions as you have time for: they might give different answers! The idea is to get a clear picture of how the equipment is used, and what impact it has had on the firm which is using it.

Task 5

Now devise a display of the information you have collected. This might take the form of a frieze, with panels of writing and photographs at important points along the process, or you might prefer to make a booklet with your photographs set in among the writing. However you present the information, it should be easy to understand, attractive and accurate.

If you decide to produce a booklet, try to show the finished material to the people in the company you visited. They will be interested in what you have done and pleased that you have taken the trouble to show them the finished product.

_____IMPORTANT_____

Read these information pages:
C Presenting information
I Computer uses

14 Customer complaints

AIM

To develop your
- skills in identifying particular roles and their effect on behaviour
- oral communication skills

Introduction

In manufacture a great deal of time and money is spent in ensuring that all the goods despatched are of a high quality. Cars, for example, are inspected along the production line to ensure that any fault is quickly located and corrected. Televisions are checked for picture quality using the test card. Samples of some goods are even tested to destruction, to ensure that the customer has good value for money.

Inevitably, however, faults do occur, and people in the manufacturing trade have to learn to deal with complaints. This assignment takes the form of a role-play.

Figure 1 First situation

Ashvin Patel

Ashvin Patel is a 31-year-old sales assistant for a small firm making personal files for the business person. Ashvin has been working at the firm for 16 months, but is rather unhappy as recently a new employee was promoted after only 3 months to Field Supervisor, a job which Ashvin hoped to get.

One particular morning is very busy. A new consignment of paper has been left in the salesroom due to storage problems, and the young assistant in the salesroom is moving this to a more permanent storeroom. The firm's sales area is under-staffed at the moment, due to an unfilled vacancy for a junior assistant.

The lunch-break starts at 12.45. At 12.30 a customer called Mrs Moreland comes into the shop and complains that the file pages stick together and are very difficult to turn. Ashvin is very impatient with her and snatches the file from her, muttering that other people have had no difficulty turning pages. Following a brief exchange of words, the customer loses her temper and asks to see the Manager. At this point, Ashvin tries to calm things down, but Mrs Moreland is very upset and demands to see the Manager.

During the discussion with the Manager it is discovered that Mrs Moreland came to the firm yesterday lunchtime and found the salesroom closed, and that she made a special effort to bring the file back today as she was going on a conference tomorrow and wanted the file to take with her.

Task 1

Read Figure 1, and then discuss these points:

(a) What factors caused the situation to become out of hand?
(b) How should Ashvin Patel have handled the situation?
(c) What could the Manager do in Mrs Moreland's case?
(d) What action should the Manager take with regard to Ashvin?
(e) What factors are in Ashvin's favour, if any?

Figure 2 Second situation

> **Willtime Clocks**
>
> Willtime Clocks is a firm making made-to-measure wall clocks for major office situations. The business prides itself on the importance it gives to customer goodwill and reflects this in an exchange policy for faulty goods. Due to the delicate nature of the clocks, however, it will not refund money on returns for other reasons. This policy is a key feature in training for all staff members. The only person able to make exceptions to the policy is the manager, and then only in very special circumstances.

Figure 3 Role card

> **Mr Waterhouse − customer**
>
> You are 41 years old. You work at a local firm which makes chairs for schools.
>
> You purchased the wall clock for your wife's birthday present. There is a particular area in your kitchen which you felt would be just right for the clock. This area is between two fitted bottle-storage areas. You saw the clock when passing the shop, and bought it on the assumption that it would fit in the area intended. Mrs Broom, the sales assistant, sold you the clock over two weeks ago, just before you went away with your wife on holiday.
>
> When you got home that day, you tried the clock in the area for which it was intended but found that it would not fit. You then decided to return the clock after your holiday.
>
> This particular afternoon you have returned the clock, a little anxious about the time between purchase and bringing back the clock. You are most upset when the firm refuse to give you a refund due both to the policy of the firm and to the time lapse between the purchase of the goods and their return.
>
> Try to persuade the shop assistant to give you a refund, and to do so today.

Task 2

Read Figure 2. In pairs, take the two roles (Figures 3 and 4) and play out the scene.

Figure 4 Role card

> ### Mrs Broom − sales assistant
>
> You are 20 years old, and have been working at Willtime Clocks for 1 year 3 months. You know that on some occasions customers have returned clocks, only for the firm to find that the clocks have been damaged in various ways. The general policy is *not* to exchange goods but for customer goodwill you do sometimes exchange the goods or refund the money. This decision, however, is normally made because of future custom the particular purchaser could bring to the firm. It is usually made by the manager. You get on very well with the manager of the firm, Linda Miles, but you feel that she sometimes lets the customer get away with too much.
>
> On this particular afternoon a customer calls into your salesroom to return a clock purchased two weeks ago, which does not fit an area in his kitchen for which it was intended. It is Linda's day off and you have to deal with this yourself.
>
> Try to resolve the situation to the satisfaction of the firm. Bear in mind that you will have to justify your decision to Linda Miles on her return tomorrow.

Task 3

As a group, discuss these questions:

(a) How did it feel to be in the situation of the customer and of the sales assistant?

(b) What points could the firm include in their policy statement which would assist in dealing with any future complaints of this nature?

(c) Is Mr Waterhouse entitled to a refund? (You might like to find out the *legal* position regarding a refund of goods.)

——IMPORTANT——

Read this information page:
F Role-playing

15 Shape up

To develop your

- ability to design an item for a purpose
- problem-solving skills
- skills in presenting information

Introduction

The ability to adjust the position of the driver's seat is just one of the many features included in the design of all cars, but it is very important. The mechanism which adjusts the seat is usually adequate for most drivers.

This assignment involves you firstly in finding out *how* car seats are adjusted, and secondly in designing a mechanism suited to the needs of a particular driver.

Task 1

Examine several cars and consider how the seat mechanism works.

Sketch the mechanism in *two* different vehicles and explain the operation. Include in your report:

(a) an explanation of why seats are required to move;
(b) the measurements of both mechanisms, in terms of total movement from fully back to fully forward;
(c) details of how any other adjustment of the seat is made.

Task 2

A small driver complains that the car seat will not move close enough to the steering wheel for driving to be comfortable. Choose *one* of the mechanisms considered in Task 1 and design a modified version of the unit.

Task 3

Think about safety and the driving position using the modified seat mechanism. Can you recommend any other features which should be the subject of re-design, e.g. the interior mirror or any of the switches? Include any recommendations in your report.

Task 4

If you have access to a suitable workshop you could actually manu-facture the re-designed seat mechanism.

──IMPORTANT──

Read these information pages:
A Properties of
   materials
E Health and safety

16 A bench for all seasons

AIM

To develop your
- ability to design a product
- experience in costing a product
- understanding of simple business procedure
- ability to manufacture a product

Introduction

At all times of the year you may see people sitting quite comfortably on wooden benches, either in parks or in their own gardens. Some of these people will have purchased their bench, and may have found them expensive.

Yet the benches are quite simple to make. This assignment asks you to design a wooden bench and to produce an inventory of the materials and processes needed in its manufacture. You are asked to consider the setting up of a mini-business venture making such benches. You will therefore need to find out how much they cost to make, in time and material, and to look at the costs incurred in running a business. You will also need to include some profit margin.

Task 1

Begin by taking some measurements on which to base your bench design. The size of the seat you are sitting on will be a guide, but it would be better to go and measure some actual benches.

Make a rough drawing which shows all these measurements. Decide whether the bench is to seat two or three people, and adjust the sizes on your design accordingly.

Task 2

Look at the ways benches are constructed, and decide how yours will be built. Remember that the bench may be outside in all weathers and so may need extra strength to withstand the seasons of the year.

Consider the sizes of the pieces of wood to be used, and include these on your drawing. Are you going to use wood of the same-size section for both the main structures and the seat laths?

Task 3

In order to keep the cost down, you will need to use the least amount of wood possible consistent with your design. Consider and report on what *is* the least amount of wood you will need.

Task 4

Calculate the total cost of this wood, by contacting or visiting a timber merchant. The firm may also be able to advise you about protection of the wood with paint or varnish, and so on. Include these costs in your report.

Task 5

Estimate the time it will take you to make each bench, from the time you purchase the wood to the finished product. Convert this into a cost per hour. Your tutor will help you with this exercise and show you how to make the estimate fairly accurate.

Task 6

If a workshop is available, make the bench, either as a group or as an individual. A tutor in the woodwork shop may be able to assist in this matter of production.

Compare the process of making the bench as a group or as an individual: what advantages could be gained by either manufacturing process? You should remember that in a real business, orders might be taken and you might need to make a large number of these benches. Time might be very important.

Task 7

Compile a report on the exercise, including a diagram of the bench with details of its size. Include the suggested final price of each bench.

Have you identified any improvements you could make? You could also include in your report a marketing strategy to show how you would attempt to gain some initial orders for your benches.

_____IMPORTANT_____

Read these information pages:
C Presenting
   information
J Costs

17 Save your energy

___AIM___

To develop your
- ability to carry out surveys and organise findings
- understanding of energy efficiency
- knowledge of energy usage
- skills in presenting information

Introduction

A large factor in the cost of producing manufactured goods is the energy used to make them. In many manufacturing companies these costs are higher than necessary because energy is used inefficiently. This damages the profits of the company; it is also wasteful, and energy in the world is in limited supply.

This assignment should be completed during the work-experience part of your programme. While doing it you will learn about the different energy supplies used by your placement company, the cost, and sources of energy inefficiency. You will also have a chance to consider a company code of practice for the efficient use of energy.

Task 1

Find the names and addresses of main suppliers of energy in your region.

Contact your local gas and electricity boards, and collect information about prices of energy, both to manufacturing companies and to domestic consumers. Each board will be able to provide you with information (perhaps as leaflets) on saving energy.

If you think you need further background information on saving energy, carry out your own research in the library or invite a speaker from the gas or electricity board.

It may help you to draw together your research findings if you write a report for your own use later.

Task 2

Identify all the sources of energy used by your work-experience placement. Who supplies it, and how? It may help to record this basic information in a grid such as the one in Figure 1.

Figure 1 Energy sources

ENERGY SOURCE	SUPPLIER	METHOD OF SUPPLY
Gas	West Midlands Gas Board	Dedicated pipes (gas mains)

Task 3

You will now need to find out how much the company pays for the different kinds of energy it uses during the year. Arrange an interview with the company manager to obtain this information. It would be useful to find out the total costs for each kind of energy, and the cost per unit to the firm.

How does the firm's energy use change over the year? Why is this? It might help to plot the quarterly change in the cost of energy through the year as a graph or bar chart.

Task 4

Carry out a survey of the company to identify what equipment, machines, and processes (heating, lighting, etc.) use what kinds of energy.

Using the basic research carried out in Task 1, make a list of all the energy-inefficient practices you observe in the company, in relation to each piece of equipment, machine or process. What do employees do which may waste energy? How is the work organised?

Task 5

A code of practice is simply a list of things to do to minimise a particular problem. Write a code of practice designed to help people understand how they can save energy. Include guidelines for the managers of the work placement, who often control how the work is done and the environment in which people work.

Task 6

Arrange a meeting with the work-placement manager to present your findings. Explain the use of the energy-saving code and ask for comments. Find out the manager's views on the work you have done, and whether he or she thinks the code would save energy in the company.

Task 7

When you return from your work experience, present your findings and the energy-saving code of practice to your tutor and group.

———IMPORTANT———

Read these information pages:
C Presenting
   information
D Sources of
   information
J Costs

18 Mushroom-growing

AIM

To develop your skills in
- researching information
- planning and organising
- monitoring a manufacturing programme
- recording experiences

Introduction

Mushrooms are a popular food, and many households buy them regularly for use in cooked meals and salads. This assignment aims to increase your understanding of small-batch manufacture and its place in the local economy. You will be buying mushroom kits, growing crops and selling them to local retailers. The assignment will involve you in using research skills, planning and organising skills, arranging and making visits, and setting up and monitoring an economically viable manufacturing programme.

Task 1

Start by finding out as much as you can about local retailers who sell mushrooms, from the larger supermarket to the small corner shop. Try to find out the quantity of mushrooms each retail outlet sells in a week. Enter your results in a table.

Task 2

Who are the growers? Where are they located?

Use *Yellow Pages* and other information sources to identify suppliers, as well as talking to retailers. Use a large-scale local map to record locations.

Task 3

Arrange a visit to a mushroom grower, and keep records of what you find out. It would be helpful if you could take photographs.

Prepare a presentation for your group to show what you have found out.

Task 4

Now that you have a clear idea of your target market and of what mushroom-growing involves, you are ready to start production.

Find out who sells mushroom-growing kits locally (e.g. gardening centres or large DIY stores). Compare prices. Note the information on packs about the time it will take for the mushroom to crop, and the promised yield per pack. Calculate the price you will need to charge to recover your outlay on the kits and to make a profit.

Task 5

(a) Survey potential sales and estimate the number of mushroom kits you will need.
(b) Find out about schemes for borrowing money for school or college enterprises. Arrange to borrow start-up capital.
(c) Identify a suitable location for growing your crops.

Task 6

Purchase your mushroom kits and begin manufacture, keeping detailed records of:

(a) the number of crops per kit;
(b) the weight per crop and per kit;
(c) the effects on production of differing conditions;
(d) any necessary price adjustments;
(e) your sales and profits.

Task 7

After an agreed period, wind up the business and prepare a detailed report. Comment on:

(a) your preparation and research;
(b) your analysis of production and sales;
(c) your problems, successes, and conclusions.

———— IMPORTANT ————

Read these information pages:

B Social-survey techniques
C Presenting information
D Sources of information
J Costs

19 Spillage

To develop your
- awareness of health-and-safety regulations
- skills in working in a group
- ability to interpret graphs
- ability to collect and present information

Introduction

A huge number of chemicals are used in manufacture, many of them being dangerous. In the workplace steps can be taken to protect workers and to prevent accidents, but these hazardous chemicals are also transported from one place to another, by road or rail.

In the event of an accident, the emergency services need to know what to do — what the hazards are and how to deal with them. This depends on the type of chemical. To help with this, each chemical now has a unique and internationally agreed UN number. Whatever the trade name of the chemical product being transported, the numbers say what chemicals it contains. In addition, vehicles carrying hazardous chemicals now display *Hazchem* signs which make clear what sort of chemicals are involved. The codes on the Hazchem sign tell the emergency services what action to take.

This assignment considers the transport of hazardous chemicals and the dangers involved.

Figure 1 The Hazchem code

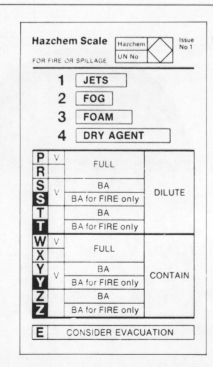

51

Task 1

Look at Figure 1, which shows a Hazchem scale card and the accompanying notes.

As a group, make a survey of the chemicals transported in your neighbourhood. You will need to monitor the traffic on various roads. Choose:

(a) a range of locations − e.g. industrial estates, housing developments, trunk roads, streets in towns, streets in residential areas;
(b) a range of times of day − the rush hour, mid-morning, lunchtime, evening, and so on.

Figure 2 Transport of hazardous chemicals

You may like to divide into sub-groups, each sub-group being responsible for a different part of the survey. Record your observations in a table (Figure 2).

Vehicles carrying chemicals					
NUMBER	HAZCHEM BOARD DISPLAYED?	UN CODE DISPLAYED?	HAZCHEM CODE No.	HAZARD No.	EMERGENCY TREATMENT
1					
2					

Task 2

Meet in sub-groups and gather together all your observations. Produce a brief summary of your findings, saying:

(a) the area concerned;
(b) the number of vehicles identified;
(c) the percentage carrying Hazchem boards;
(d) the chemicals carried;
(e) the action to be taken in an emergency.

Task 3

Each sub-group needs copies of the reports of all the other sub-groups.

Put together the results from the different sub-groups to make a clear overall report. This should explain how and where the survey took place, present your findings, and identify the dangers.

Task 4

Send a copy of your report to your local police force. In an accompanying letter, say how the survey came to be made and how it fits into your course. Invite comments on your findings and ask for further information about hazardous chemicals.

_____IMPORTANT_____

Read these information pages:
C Presenting information
E Health and safety
H Technical terms

20 Packaging problems

AIM

To develop your
- knowledge of the role of packaging in marketing
- skills in designing with given materials
- skills in identifying market demand
- skills in presenting information clearly

Introduction

The first time most people see a manufactured product is when it is completely finished and in its packaging. Packaging is of vital importance to the success of a product, particularly a new product, and a great deal of time and money goes into its design. Packaging must be safe, secure and must advertise and promote the product.

Different products require different styles of packaging, and the packaging must also be functional: it must contain the product safely while it is being transported, it must not leak, and it must keep the contents in the best condition for the customer. A clever and simple example of this is the way air is blown into crisp bags so that the crisps inside are protected.

This assignment gives you the chance to try to design and produce an example of good packaging.

Task 1

Think of a product that is suitable for this assignment. A simple idea will be the best, for example a new chocolate bar or washing powder; anything that needs packaging will do.

Now go out to shops which sell similar items and look at the current range of packaging. Try to collect examples from home or from friends, and look at the design of the wrapping. Try to decide what age group, sex, income level and personality the producers are aiming at. All of these elements will have been discussed when the packaging was designed.

Task 2

Talk to your friends and parents about their preferences and decide what your new product will be. Write down the new features and benefits of your product, and try to decide on the sorts of people who might eventually be interested in buying it.

Write a description of your product as clearly as you can, and describe a typical customer. Think about this person and write down the sort of packaging that might appeal to them. Why will your product attract them? How will the packaging help to persuade them to buy the product?

Task 3

Draw up three possible examples of packaging and colour them. Make sure that you include on the wrapping the details of the contents,

the weight, the manufacturer's name and address, and the country of origin, as well as the product name.

Show the designs to people who are similar to your description of a possible customer, and make a note of the comments they make.

Task 4
Having selected the best visual design, think how this will look when flat. What shape will it be? How will it be folded? Look at how existing wrappers are printed and folded, and see if you can improve on them or offer a new way of approaching the problem. For example, king-sized ice-cream cones posed a problem to packagers in that the cone and the topping both needed to be covered. This was solved by using *two* pieces of paper.

_____IMPORTANT_____

Read these information
pages:
C Presenting
   information
J Costs

Task 5
Using materials available to you, create a mock-up or three-dimen-
sional model of the packaging. Write up your customer profile and
product description in a final form and add your working drawings.
Present the finished work to the other members of your group.

Information pages

Properties of materials

The importance of mechanical properties

It is very important for the engineer to understand the mechanical properties of materials and how they relate to the design or methods of production. Each material has its own range or combination of qualities and is used in particular circumstances.

Examples

(a) On a bicycle there are parts which have to withstand a great deal of stress and wear – the chain wheel, chain, sprockets and bearings. These require a hard and wear-resistant metal.

(b) Electric cables need to conduct electricity. They also need to be flexible so that they can turn corners and withstand movement.

(c) Cooking pans need to be made from a material which will resist heat.

(d) Bed springs require metal that can deform and then return to its original shape.

(e) Road springs on vehicles need to withstand large and repeated loads and shocks during their lifetime.

(f) Bolts need to stretch and to withstand considerable stress.

Forces acting on materials

When a force acts upon a material it can stretch, compress or shear it, as shown in Figure 1.

Figure 1 Types of force

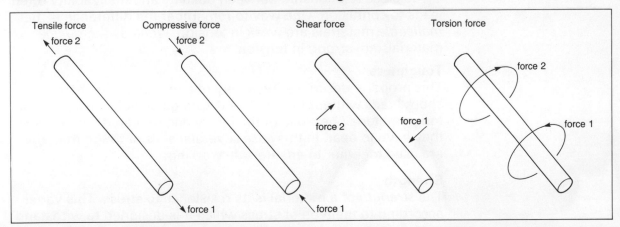

Principal mechanical properties

Ductility

Ductility is a measure of a material's ability to be 'cold worked' without fracturing. A ductile material can be stretched or drawn out. It is permanently deformed when drawn out, and does not return to its original size as an *elastic* material would.

There is a close relationship between 'ductility' and 'malleability'. Make sure you understand the difference between these properties.

Brittleness

A *brittle* material will break easily when deformed. Glass is very brittle: a very small deformation of the material results in its fracture.

Hardness

Hard materials resist wear. Hardness is measured by placing a steel ball onto the material to be tested. After a certain load, the mark or indentation in the material is measured. The smaller the indentation made, the harder the material.

Elasticity

Elastic materials (such as rubber bands) stretch, but return to their original size when released. Each elastic material, however, has an *elastic limit*: when this limit is exceeded, the material will fracture.

Malleability

Malleability is similar to ductility. In this case, however, compressive forces (rather than stretching forces) are brought to bear on the material. These forces include hammering or rolling. The material is permanently deformed: it does not return to its original shape when released.

The close relationship between ductility and malleability often leads to confusion. One way to remember the difference is that *malleable* materials are *weak* in tension, whereas the *ductile* materials are *strong* in tension.

Toughness

This property describes the ability of a material to withstand shock loads without fracture. Leaf springs on vehicles require a tough material, because of the heavy and repeated shock loads they have to bear. In this case several leaves of tough material are used together to ensure safe working.

Strength

The *strength* of a material is its resistance to stress. This varies according to the type of stress which it is designed to withstand – tension, compression, shear forces, and so on.

Social-survey techniques

Uses

Social surveys in the form of questionnaires and public-opinion interviews have become a common technique of gathering information both in industry and by social scientists.

Purposes
In industry and commerce, survey techniques are used to monitor customer reaction to, and opinion on, a wide variety of issues – for example the colour and shape of packaging or the effectiveness of a particular advertising campaign.

Kinds of survey
The most common forms of survey techniques used are:
(a) *promotional campaigns* – for example the distribution of products to a selected area in order to assess customer opinion, or the use of free samples for the same purpose;
(b) *questionnaires* – these are used for gathering more detailed information about peoples' reactions or opinions; and
(c) *interviews* – this survey technique is not common in industry or commerce, and is mainly used when detailed or selective information is sought.
In this information page we will concentrate on the use of questionnaires.

Usual format

The public-opinion questionnaire can be used for a variety of purposes such as the assessment of peoples' political views or social attitudes, as well as to discover product preferences.
   The questionnaire consists of a series of structured questions designed to draw from the interviewee specific answers.
   To achieve this structure in a questionnaire, it is necessary to follow a certain procedure. The procedure can be divided into six stages.

Stage 1: Survey design
(a) You must first decide what it is you wish to find out.
(b) Then you have to decide on the number and type (for example, the age, sex and occupation) of people who you

think will be able to supply the required information, or be representative of such groups.

(c) Next you must choose the wording and order of the questions. The main problems to watch out for at this stage are these.

- *Wording* It is possible with questionnaires to word a question in such a way that you get the answer you expected. For example the quesiton, 'Do you think the Government should go to war to defend the liberty and freedom of its subjects?' would probably draw from interviewees a positive response to going to war. Whereas a question such as 'Should the Government go to war on behalf of another country?' would probably draw the opposite reply.

- *Bias* This is reflected not only in the wording used, as in the example above, but also in the way questions are constructed. By quoting figures of authority in questions, the interviewer is probably introducing bias into that question. People tend to respect authority and would not normally wish to be seen in contradiction to it. For example, 'Would you agree with the opinion of the majority of doctors that smoking should be banned in public places?' (rather than 'Do you think smoking should be banned in public places?').

- *Ambiguity* It is important to avoid the use of questions that are vaguely worded and that can therefore be interpreted in more than one way. For example, 'Are you in favour of government policies that affect old people?' is ambiguous because a 'yes' answer could be given for two reasons. The interviewee could mean that he or she is in favour of active policies in general, even though he or she feels that the existing policies affect old people negatively. The answer would also be 'yes' if the interviewee felt such policies affected old people positively.

- *Selecting questions* Here it is important to decide on the nature of the response you are seeking. In questionnaires there are two main types of questions: *closed questions* restrict the answer that can be given to either a 'yes' or 'no' answer, or to placing a tick in the appropriate box; *open questions* allow interviewees to answer in their own words. Each type has advantages and disadvantages. On the whole, closed questions are much easier to analyse but much more difficult to construct. In most questionnaires a mixture of both types is used.

- *Personal questions* In a general questionnaire, try to avoid too many personal questions, as people do not like answering such questions. If you do need to ask them, try to keep them indirect (closed questions are best for this). For example:

'How old are you?'
please tick box:

☐ under 18

☐ 18 to 35

☐ 36 to 55

☐ over 56

- *Order of questions* When designing a questionnaire, try to group questions of a similar nature together. This not only makes the progression more logical when answering, but helps later at the analysis stage.

Stage 2: Sample survey
In order to assess the soundness of a questionnaire a sample survey is normally conducted. This entails trying out the questionnaire on a proportion of the total sample.

As your time will probably be limited, we suggest that you try your questionnaire out on a few fellow students to see if it contains any structural problems. If it does then you will need to make the necessary alterations before conducting your full-scale survey.

Stage 3: Conducting the survey
There are three basic ways in which a survey based on a questionnaire can be conducted:
(a) selecting a sample group of people and then sending them a questionnaire by post, asking for completion and return;
(b) stopping a selection of appropriate people in the street and asking them to fill in your questionnaire there and then;
(c) the same as (b), but with the interviewer asking the questions and writing the answers on the questionnaire form.

The type of procedure you use will depend on the sorts of questions you are asking; people do not liked to be asked too many personal questions in the street but they might answer if the questions are sent to them privately through the post.

Each method has its own advantages and disadvantages. The main problem with method (a) is that there is normally a very high non-response rate. This could mean that your survey becomes biased because only a selective group of people respond.

Stage 4: Classifying the information

Once the survey has been conducted, some analysis of the results is necessary. Before this analysis can take place, the answers to the questions have to be classified; in other words, you have to examine the replies you have received and categorise them under headings or titles. With closed questions this is easy because all you have to do is count up the number of ticks or 'yes/no' answers. Categorising can sometimes be made easy by using the actual question in the survey as the title for your classification.

Stage 5: Data analysis

Once you have classified your data it is then possible to analyse it – that is, you will be able to look at the results and see clearly the conclusions you can draw. What these conclusions will be depends largely on the type of questions asked and the people interviewed.

Stage 6: Presenting your results

It is important to present your conclusions clearly and logically. This can be done by the use of statistical data, by graphical presentation, or by presenting them verbally or in a written report. The choice of presentation will depend on:
(a) the type and nature of questionnaire; and
(b) the nature of the audience being informed of your results.

For information on the presentation of statistical data, see information page D.

Here is an example of a questionnaire on present and future UK energy resources.

This survey's aim is to discover the public's awareness of present and future UK Energy resources: to find out the public's attitudes and reactions to the energy crisis.

OCCUPATION: _____

SEX: ☐ Male   ☐ Female

AGE: ☐ 16–20   ☐ 31–40   ☐ 51–60
      ☐ 21–30   ☐ 41–50   ☐ 60+

---

1. Which form of energy do you think generates the greatest proportion of electricity into the National Grid?

   ☐ Gas   ☐ Nuclear
   ☐ Oil   ☐ HEP (Hydroelectric power)
   ☐ Coal   ☐ Others

2. Which of the following do you think consumes most energy in this country?

   ☐ Iron and steel industry   ☐ Domestic
   ☐ Industry (others)   ☐ Others
   ☐ Transportation

3. Are you in favour of nuclear energy production?

   ☐ YES   ☐ NO   ☐ UNDECIDED

4. Which of the following 'alternative' energy sources have you heard of?

   ☐ Wind   ☐ Geothermal
   ☐ Solar   ☐ Plants
   ☐ Ocean Thermal   (eg Water-Hyacinth)
     Energy Conversion   ☐ Splitting hydrogen
   ☐ Tidal   ☐ Others _____
                                  _____

5. Which of the previous list do you consider would be the most realistic future alternative energy source for the UK?

   _____
   _____
   _____

6. Do you consider that the following are vital to UK energy production?

   Natural Gas   Coal   Oil
   ☐ YES   ☐ YES   ☐ YES
   ☐ NO   ☐ NO   ☐ NO
   ☐ UNDECIDED   ☐ UNDECIDED   ☐ UNDECIDED

7. Do you have central heating? ☐ YES ☐ NO

   If YES please tick one of the following
   ☐ Oil   ☐ Electricity
   ☐ Gas   ☐ Other _____
   ☐ Solid fuel   _____

8. Have you ever seriously considered the use of Solar Panels at home?

   ☐ YES ☐ NO
   If YES, what did you eventually decide and why?

   _____

   _____
   _____
   _____

9. Do you consider that an energy conservation policy should be an important consideration of our Government?

   ☐ YES ☐ NO ☐ UNDECIDED

10. Have you taken any steps towards conservation in your own home?

    ☐ YES ☐ NO
    If YES please tick which of the following

    ☐ Loft insulation   ☐ Draught-stripping
    ☐ Cavity wall insulation   ☐ System controls
    ☐ Hot water tank insulation   ☐ Double-glazing

    ☐ Others _____

    _____

11. Did you receive a local government grant for any of the above?

    ☐ YES ☐ NO

Presenting information

A lot of the work in this book asks you to research topics and collect information. You then need to record the information, for your own use some time later or in order to communicate it to someone else.

Writing is one way of presenting information, but in service engineering it is often not the best way. Below are some notes about other methods.

Questions about presentation

Before deciding *how* to present your information, ask yourself these questions:

(a) What kind of information do I want to present? (For example, you might want to show numerical data or talk about personal experiences.)

(b) Who do I want to see and understand the information? (For example, is it for your tutor to see, or for visitors to your school or college?)

(c) How could someone misunderstand the information? (For example, will your audience be able to see what a diagram is illustrating?)

(d) What will the audience do with the information? (For example, will they assess your findings or carry out some task according to your instructions?)

Spend some time thinking about and answering these questions. They will help you to present the information in a way that is both accurate and effective.

Guidelines

The following rules are a useful guide when considering how to give information to someone else:

(a) be neat and tidy;
(b) be logical;
(c) be clear and precise;
(d) be simple;
(e) make it interesting;
(f) show where you got the information from.

Methods of presentation

Writing

A common fault is to present different kinds of information in the same way. Too often we *write* what we want to communicate. Writing can be very effective for some material, but it is often an inappropriate and an uninteresting way of giving facts, figures, and experiences.

Visual displays

It is often better to present information visually than to write a description. Compared with writing, visual presentations can have greater

(a) impact;
(b) interest;
(c) clarity.

On the other hand, visual presentations

(a) may over-simplify the facts;
(b) may not be an easy way to present arguments.

Kinds of visual presentation

Drawings

Drawings can be very useful for showing your own ideas and experiences and for presenting complex information. Figure 1 shows an example.

Figure 1

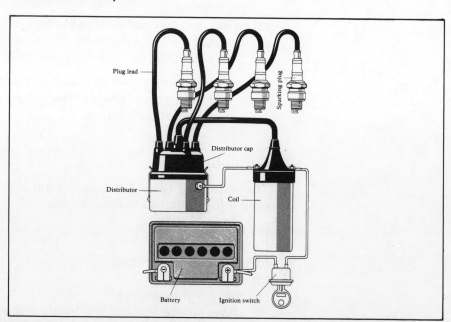

Staged drawings

Very often the most effective way of giving instructions for a complicated task is to show it in several stages, as in Figure 2. Each stage of the task should be clearly numbered and described.

Figure 2

Clearing a blocked basin with a plunger

When a sink, bath or basin is blocked, it may be necessary to dismantle the trap below it; but first try to clear it with a plunger.

Note that if a lavatory pan is blocked, a special type of plunger is needed (see p. 159).

Material: rag.
Tools: plunger; cup or mug.

Plunger

1 Push a rag into the basin overflow hole so that air and water cannot escape when plunger is used

2 Take out sufficient water from the basin to prevent slopping over when the plunger is used

3 Place a plunger firmly over the waste outlet hole. Work the handle vigorously up and down

4 When the blockage is dislodged, the pool of water will drain out. Turn on a tap and agitate the plunger

5 Remove rag from the overflow hole and run cold water for a minute or two to refill the trap

Diagrams and plans

These are useful for presenting information and relationships that would be hard to communicate in words (as in Figure 3). Always make sure that diagrams are clearly labelled.

Figure 3

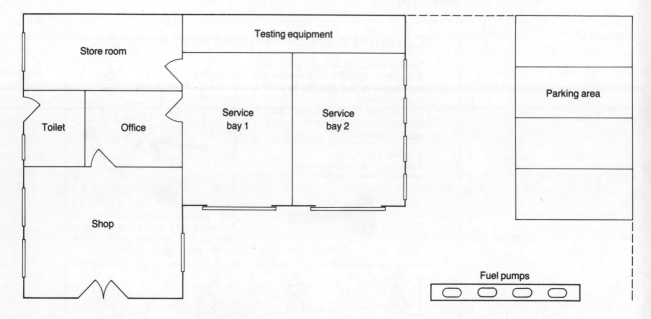

Photographs

Photographs allow real-life situations to be shown to the viewer. They may have the greatest visual impact. Sometimes, though, diagrams may be clearer. The diagram in Figure 4 is probably easier to understand than a photograph of the same object would be.

Figure 4

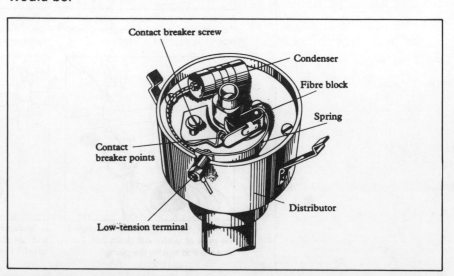

Figure 5

Cuttings

There is a lot of information in newspapers and magazines. It may be a good idea to cut some of these out and keep them for future reference. (See Figure 5.)

TUNERS—THE FAULTS WE FOUND

The columns show the number of tuners or garages making each kind of mistake

		Tuners	Garages	All
Air filter	– not checked; not replaced or cleaned	6	5	11
Air cleaner case	– not set to correct winter/summer position	2	4	6
	– not clipped down properly; pipe not connected	2	0	2
Carburettor	– CO content incorrect	13	15	28
	– dashpot overfilled	6	2	8
	– idle speed too low or too high	3	4	7
	– fuel leak not fixed or reported	0	1	1
	– choke cable frayed, not reported	1	0	1
	– throttle cable out of adjustment, not reported	0	1	1
Ignition	– timing advanced/retarded, not checked	4	7	11
	– spark plugs not cleaned; not set correctly; over-tightened; not replaced; wrong type fitted	4	4	8
	– dwell angle wrong, excessive variation	2	2	4
	– leads faulty, poor connections	0	4	4

		Tuners	Garages	All
Ignition cont'd	– vacuum pipe damaged, not reported	2	1	3
	– CB contacts badly misaligned	0	2	2
	– vacuum diaphragm not working, not reported	1	0	1
	– cam lobe inaccuracy not reported	1	0	1
	– cam excessively lubricated	1	0	1
Valves	clearances not checked; not adjusted	9	13	22
	– valve cover gasket not renewed	4	0	4
	– adjusted too tightly, wrong	3	0	3
Parts replaced unnecessarily	– spark plugs	3	5	8
	– CB points	1	2	3
	– condenser	3	0	3
	– distributor cap	2	0	2
	– rotor arm	2	0	2
	– air filter element	0	1	1
	– carburettor diaphragm	0	1	1
Number of cars tuned		21	19	40

Video

You may have access to video recording and playback facilities. Video provides perhaps the most dramatic method of presenting information. Although it may be impossible to achieve the startling special effects of professional video studios, a simple domestic video recorder and camera provides an effective way of presenting real-life or simulated-action events.

Perhaps the most single important drawback to video presentation is the time it takes. You should allocate at least several hours to the production of even a two-minute sequence of video action. Planning, selecting, finding or setting up the location, writing the script, filming, and editing all make great demands on time and effort.

Tape recording

Tape recording offers another way of presenting information. It is less time-consuming than video, but still requires considerable planning. Sound recording is especially useful and appropriate when you have obtained your information from recorded interviews and you wish to present extracts rather than to write out what was said.

Sources of information

Information is a general term for the facts without which our complicated modern world would grind to a halt. There is now so much information in the world that it is impossible for any one person ever to know it all, or even to know where all of it can be found.

Those who have information (or access to it) may have power. But information itself has no value unless it can be used. Knowing how to find out what you want to know is therefore a very useful skill.

Sources of information

Information is all around us. For example, there are information centres in every town. There are libraries, tourist information offices, council offices, Citizens' Advice Bureaux, chambers of trade, police stations, bookstalls and newsagents, bus and railway stations.

Where do you start?
The largest source of information is the people in the community. People are usually very willing to help. For example, you may feel that your doctor is only available when you are ill, and your bank manager only when you want a loan, but they will usually be very helpful if you approach them with questions about their own specialist areas. The business community too is a rich source of knowledge, skills and experience.

If you don't know the names or addresses of local sources, the best place to start is a library. Your own school or college probably has a well-equipped library of its own; if not, try the local town library. The town libraries will probably have an information desk or an information section.

Getting information

Asking
One good way of finding things out is to ask other people. This may not be easy if you are shy, but if you can develop your confidence in asking for help you will find that many other things you do will become easier.

Looking

How much do you know about the firms that are trading in your town? Almost every side street will have some employer carrying out some commercial activity. As you walk around, start paying attention to these areas.

You may have an industrial estate near you – a place where several firms that need manufacturing or workshop space operate next to one another. Take a walk around one – you'll be surprised at the variety of companies there.

Reading

There are now many directories that list the names of firms and what they do. Your local library information section will contain a large number of such trade directories. The most commonly available is the *Yellow Pages* (Figure 1). Chambers of commerce and other business organisations produce lists of their members, as do many county councils.

Figure 1

Chambers of trade, chambers of commerce and chambers of commerce and industry differ in their national organisation, but they are all voluntary associations of businesses. Each will have a local secretary who will be a very useful contact if you want to get in touch with local firms. Local newspapers usually have special sections giving the names of local service and repair companies, and many local councils produce lists of local services.

Writing
You may want to visit, or get information from, a local organisation or firm. Business people are busy, and to begin with it may be best to write. Say clearly in your letter what you want to do or find out, and make the letter as neat as you can manage – the employer will get his or her first impression of you from your letter.

Most organisations are used to receiving inquiries from students, and they may send you more material than you expected.

Listening
If you arrange an interview, plan carefully so that you make the best use of the time. Write your questions down before the interview so that you don't overlook any area of interest to you. Pay attention, be serious and be polite. Take a notepad and try to record what you are told.

Good listening is a skill in itself. The person you are interviewing will probably give you lots of information: if you are nervous or waiting to ask your next question, you will miss much of what is said. To practise listening, try interviewing another member of your group about a hobby or a holiday.

Using computers
Computers make information storage, retrieval and communication much simpler. More and more local libraries, schools and even major shops are installing computer terminals which make information available at the touch of a few buttons. The information may actually be stored on much larger computers many miles away, but it will be sent to your terminal down the telephone line, or broadcast like television programmes, perhaps even via satellite. Talking, reading, writing and listening will continue to be important, but as the amount of information available continues to grow, the use of computers will become more and more common.

Health and safety

A case study

Janet worked in a department store. One day she was asked to go to the stockroom to fetch replacement stock for her department. The box she wanted was shelved a little higher than she could reach. At the far end of the stockroom was a movable step-ladder, but Janet thought that if she stood for a moment on the bottom shelf she could just reach the box she wanted. In fact the shelf gave way, however, and Janet fell backwards. She needed stitches for a cut on the back of her head, and her right ankle was in plaster for almost two months.

Janet acted foolishly: she should not have used the shelf as a ladder, especially as the steps were available. But did she know that? Did the department store have a code of conduct for the stockroom? Had Janet been trained in the correct way of collecting stock from the shelves? Was it her job anyway?

No employee should behave in such a way as to put himself or herself, or anybody else, at risk of injury. On the other hand employers should have codes of safe practice, they should provide training for their employees and they should provide whatever equipment is necessary to protect their employees from injury.

The Health and Safety at Work Act 1974

Health and Safety at Work
etc. Act 1974

CHAPTER 37

LONDON
HER MAJESTY'S STATIONERY OFFICE
Reprinted 1975
£1·50 net

The Health and Safety at Work Act lays down the responsibilities of employers and employees in the workplace. Legislation before 1974 had tended to relate to particular industries (e.g. mines, quarries, and chemical plants): it did not cover *all* workers. The 1974 Act updated existing legislation, widened its scope to include all workers, and set up the Health and Safety Executive to make sure that the regulations in the Act are carried out.

If the safety and health measures described in the Act are not followed by employers, the employers can be heavily fined and may even have their businesses closed down until they do carry out the measures. On the other hand, if an employer provides safety equipment and trains workers in safety procedures but the employee fails to use the equipment or ignores the safety regulations, the employer cannot be held responsible for any injury incurred by that worker. Indeed failure by an employee to carry out his or her employer's safety policy can in some instances lead to dismissal.

Sources of information

The Health and Safety at Work Act 1974 is a long and detailed document. You will be able to find a copy in a public library. Parts of the Act probably relate to your school or college, and the school or college should have a safety policy – ask if you can see it. Copies of all government legislation are available from Her Majesty's Stationery Office, but these may be expensive. You can get particular sections of the Health and Safety at Work Act from the HMSO.

Under the terms of the Health and Safety at Work Act, trade unions have the right to elect safety representatives in the workplace. You can get information from individual trade unions or from local Trades Councils on their policies on Health and Safety.

The Workers Educational Association (WEA) runs courses on health and safety for Union safety representatives – the WEA could be another source of information. If you undertake any work experience the provider will instruct you early on in the firm's health and safety policy, telling you about protective clothing and equipment, the safe use of machines, fire drills, and so on. When you visit any works ask about health and safety procedures and equipment.

Making it work

The Health and Safety at Work Act on its own cannot prevent accidents or provide safe workplaces. What it does is to provide legal protection and a statutory framework. But in everyday work it is employers and employees who make the Act effective by being conscious of health and safety in the workplace and by co-operating to prevent accidents and keep to safe working practices.

F   Role-playing

Role-playing is a way of practising skills (e.g. how to talk to customers) and a way of finding out about ideas, feelings, and problems (e.g. what it is like to do someone else's job). A role-play can help you to feel more confident about dealing with a new situation by practising first.

Figure 1   Examples of role-plays

Situation	Number of roles	Roles	Task
1. John starts a job. He feels uncertain about it.	2	The new employee The manager	Manager: to reassure John
2. A customer feels that her car service has not been carried out very well. She comes to the garage to complain.	2	The customer The mechanic	Mechanic: to deal with the customer
3. A gas fitter installing central heating systems is always *telling* his assistant to do things rather than *asking*.	2	The gas fitter The gas fitter's mate	Mate: to find a way of working with this offhand fitter

Any situation that involves people can be role-played. Figure 1 shows some examples. Role-plays can serve several different purposes.

(a) The players can find out how an individual works in a group (e.g. by role-playing a trade union member during a strike).
(b) The players can practise new skills (e.g. interviewing people in the street).
(c) The players can learn to see problems from someone else's point of view (e.g. by role-playing a teacher when the class is being rowdy).

Role-playing involves *doing* something, so it can be an enjoyable way of learning.

Reviews and discussion

Perhaps the most important part of a role-play is the discussion that follows it. You should always leave time for discussion afterwards.

Some useful questions during a review are:

(a) How did I perform my role?
(b) What specific points about the situation did the role-play reveal?
(c) What things did it show about how people behave?
(d) How could I improve what I did?

A special way of reviewing is to video the role-play and then to watch the role-play as a group. The video recording helps the players to see their own behaviour more objectively.

Guidelines for role-playing

Before beginning a role-play make sure that:

(a) you understand the situation in which the role is to be performed;
(b) you understand your role (who is it? how would *you* act in that situation?);
(c) you understand the task that your character has (see Figure 1 for examples);
(d) you have whatever materials you need (e.g. pens, paper, desk and chairs);
(e) you know how long you have for the role-play;
(f) there is enough time afterwards for the review.

Repeat the role-play if you think you can learn more by doing so.

Designing your own role-plays

All role-plays are made up of:

(a) The situation in which the role is to be played. The players need to understand the general situation and the particular problem.
(b) The roles. There should be at least two roles.
(c) The task. This is the basis of the particular role-play, and describes what you hope to achieve or to find out by role-playing.

It is a good idea to write down the situation, the roles and the task. You can then be sure that everyone is clear about the role-play before you carry it out. It is sometimes helpful if each role is described on a separate 'role card' (Figure 2). This card can give the person playing the part ideas about how to play it.

Figure 2   A role card

ROLE CARD <u>GAS FITTER</u>

You are 35 years old. Your boss is pressurising

you to reduce the time you take to complete jobs. You

are not happy about training a new fitter's mate, but

you like to get on well with your workmates.

What is a role?
A role can be:

(a) a part in a play;
(b) the way someone behaves (e.g. a bossy person);
(c) the position someone has in an organisation (e.g. a teacher in a school);
(d) the job someone does (e.g. the manager in a firm).

When you are asked to play a role, think carefully about how *you* would act if you were in that position. Try to be yourself – don't pretend to be someone else.

Using flowcharts

What is a flowchart?

A flowchart is a sequence of instructions shown as a diagram. It is one way of breaking down a complex task into its component parts, including any choices that must be made. Figure 1 shows an example.

Figure 1

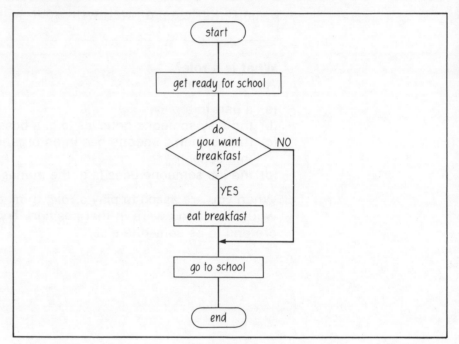

Conventions

So that other people can understand what is meant in a flowchart, certain conventions are followed in the use of shapes and the way they are joined together. It will help if you follow these as well.

Direction of flow

The main direction of flow is from the *top* of the page to the *bottom*, and from the *left* to the *right*. If a line flows up the page or from right to left, add an arrowhead to show this. Only one flowline should enter a box – if two lead to it, they should join before the box. See Figure 2.

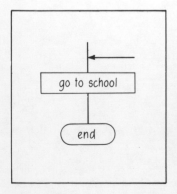

Figure 2

Shapes

Rectangular boxes are used for *statements* (often actions), and diamond-shaped ones for *questions* with a 'yes' or 'no' answer. (Each diamond should have *two* flowlines leaving it.) Parallelograms are used when *information* is taken in or given out. See Figure 3.

Beginnings and *ends* of the flow are shown as boxes with rounded ends (Figure 4).

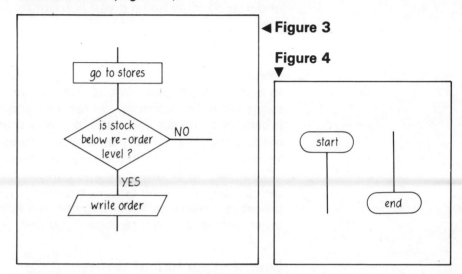

◀ **Figure 3**

Figure 4
▼

Practice

Try your hand at writing some simple flowcharts. Ask other members of your group to check that the boxes are in the right sequence. A good flowchart is easy for other people to follow.

The process of devising a well-organised flowchart will help you to think through the sequence involved in an activity.

Technical terms

In many jobs you will come across words and phrases that are new to you. You may also meet terms you thought you understood, now being given quite different meanings.

Vocational studies

In each vocational area there is a specialist vocabulary. You *need* to learn at least some of this. Tutors could remove technical terms from the teaching you receive, and work-experience providers could set you tasks in a way that avoided using them, but this would not really be kind to you as your teaching or work-experience would then be unrealistic.

You need to be attentive and curious about what's going on. Being able to use the correct names for tools, equipment or processes makes you feel happier in a new subject, and shows other people that you're committed to it.

Learning technical terms

Ask questions
Nobody will think the worse of you if you ask questions about technical terms. On the contrary, they will realise that you are taking an interest. When you hear technical terms used, try to see them written down – then any notes you make will be accurate and helpful. It is easy to mishear a term.

Use the terms
Help yourself to remember technical terms by using them in the practical situations in which they appear. If you are unsure, use a dictionary or reference book to double-check.

Keep your own list of the technical terms that are important in your vocational area. Add illustrations if these are helpful. You might like to write some of the terms on cards that you can carry in a pocket – you could look at these in spare moments. If other people are learning the same terms you could design a home-made card or board game in which technical terms have to be matched to pictures or definitions.

Jargon
Sometimes people use technical terms in unhelpful ways. They

may be trying to impress you or to bluff you into thinking they have a superior knowledge. Don't be baffled or feel put down – ask them to explain what you don't understand. You'll soon discover whether or not they know what they're talking about.

Computer uses

Any group of people who work in a specialist field develop their own special 'mini-language' or jargon. People new to the field may find these technical terms confusing, especially when a word that means one thing in everyday English means something else in the specialist use.

It is easy to be put off by people who talk in this special language. But it is important to learn some of the technical language yourself, so that you can talk accurately and without misunderstanding. The use of slang, or of incorrect terms, could lead to serious errors.

Below are some of the terms you may meet as you look at the uses of computers in manufacture.

Word processing

This is one of the most common uses of computers, and most personal computers provide word processing. Some machines do nothing but word processing and are called 'dedicated' machines; others can do other things as well.

Word processors allow you to type and store text, to move pieces of text within a document, to correct errors, and in general to work on a piece of writing which you can see on the screen until you have it as you want it. You can then save it for a later date or print it out, or both. More powerful machines can also check your spelling, combine text from different documents, or even write your letters for you!

The main components of a word processor are a keyboard, which looks just like a typewriter with some extra keys; a screen, which shows you your work; a printer, to print your work on paper; and the computer itself, which carries out the main tasks in the process.

Databases

A *database* is simply a collection of information. Many offices keep the names and telephone numbers of customers written on small cards like postcards. These are stored, usually alphabetically, in a box. This is a database. Information can be stored, changed and found easily when required.

Computers can do this very quickly, and can handle very large quantities of information that would more than fill the average office. They can also sort this information very quickly into whatever form is required — by date, by address, by telephone number, and so on. Many computer databases use the layout of a postcard file and design the screen so that the display looks like a card.

Databases can be on any subject, and may be interlinked. More powerful computers can combine data and work with word-processing programs. For example, the computer might send different standard letters to different customers, according to the information about them recorded on the database.

Spreadsheets

Another popular use of computers is in doing calculations. Many businesses need to do large quantities of calculations, particularly to keep a check on their financial situations.

For example, the accounts of a business show items of income and expenditure listed down the side and years across the top, making a grid or 'spreadsheet'. The titles and the general layout stay the same but the figures change as more money is spent or earned. Each time one figure changes, however, several calculations are needed to correct the whole grid.

With a computer-based spreadsheet you can tell the computer the calculations that need making and where the information is to be found. Then all you need to do is put in the new figures each time they change, and the computer does all the rest, automatically correcting the whole spreadsheet.

Control

Computers can also control other equipment — motors, lights, etc. They can be programmed to turn things on and off at set times, or to run motors for set periods in a certain sequence. Robot arms used in manufacturing work can be controlled by a series of instructions sent by the computer to motors which drive pistons, pulleys, gears and so on to move the arms. In manufacturing this means that a process can be carried out in exactly the same way over and over again, and the process can continue throughout the 24-hour day.

Communication

A final main use of computers is in communication. Already

there is an extensive telephone system throughout the world, and people in one place can talk to others hundreds or thousands of miles away. Now computers too can translate their information into sound and send it through the telephone system, so that documents, orders for equipment and other information can be sent very quickly over long distances.

The success of manufacturing industry is vital to any nation's success, and many companies are making increasing use of all of these uses of computers to make sure that they are able to compete effectively in today's highly competitive marketplace. Computers have a major role to play in the future success of manufacturing.

J

Costs

For all firms engaged in craft-based activities, it is essential to keep a close watch on how much an article or component costs to make. How much we sell something for is largely based on how much it costs to make.

Yet it is not always easy to take all the costs of production into account. The problem arises because there are many ways we can look at costs and measure them.

Ways of looking at costs

'How much did that item cost to make?' To answer this question fully we must include *all* the costs actually incurred in making the item.

Basically there are two types of cost: *fixed* and *variable.*

Fixed costs
Definition Costs which do not increase or decrease very much whether you make a lot of the item or only a little. (You can think of fixed costs as those costs you have to pay even if you do not make the item at all.)
Examples Rent and rates for the workshop; interest on money borrowed to buy equipment.

Variable costs
Definition Costs which *do* increase or decrease when you make more or less of the item. (You can reduce variable costs by reducing the amount of the item you make.)
Examples Costs of raw materials; wages; heating bills.

Total costs
Definition All the costs incurred in making something: the sum of the fixed costs and the variable costs.

Average costs
Definition The total costs divided by the number of things we make. It is sometimes called the 'unit cost' or the 'cost per unit'.
Use This is a very useful way of looking at cost. You can increase the unit cost by a given percentage (a 'mark-up') to pay for the skills needed to run the business. The marked-up cost is the price at which you sell each item.

Example of costs

Here are some of the important costs:
- rent
- rates
- heating
- lighting
- fuel
- raw materials
- interest on loans
- mortgage payments
- transport
- postage and telephone
- wages

Hidden costs

Some costs are hidden. Take the case of a man setting up his own business with £1000 of his own money. He doesn't actually pay anyone anything, but if he had left the £1000 in the bank or building society it would have earned interest. The lost interest is a hidden cost. *All* costs should be accounted for.

Keeping records

A golden rule for all businesses, large and small, is to keep *all* documents relating to buying and selling and to keep an accurate record of *all* transactions. Today small businesses can often afford small computers on which all this information can be stored as a database or combined as a spreadsheet.